"Pam demonstrates that the necessity of m〈 anxiety can ease another person's fear and 〈 the tension between leaving what is safe, loving, and familiar, while at the same time transitioning into what is uncertain, frightening, yet still loving. The truth she deeply and experientially captures is the importance of movement, humility, and courage in the face of fear and anxiety. She shows that as fears are faced, they seem to become smaller, less intimidating, quieter. It is a realization that fears do not have to paralyze us; it is trusting that God is present with you not only when He called you to the big picture of adoption, but that He is also present in the little moments of uncertainty. . . . It is a glimpse into the beauty of adoption, where a stranger becomes family."

—Phil Prewette, LMFT,
Licensed Marriage & Family Therapist

"I admire parents who embark on the daring adventure of adoption—becoming forever-families for a child in need. It's not usually easy, and it's not without risk. In Pam Ogden's heart-touching new adoption memoir, *He Made Me Brave*, you'll be challenged by the author's raw honesty and real love. True courage is not living without fear; it's simply the willingness to face those fears and to move forward, by faith. Pam shares memories of her first adoption experience, and the book's proceeds are raising funds for her family's second adoption. How cool is that?! If you're considering adoption, or if you desire to support the needs of one family's adoption, I encourage you to consider *He Made Me Brave*."

—Ann Dunagan,
Author and Missions Leader, MissionMindedFamilies.org

"As the father of six children, two of whom are adopted, I've often referred to the process of adoption as a 'conception we can observe outside of the body.' Twists, turns, dead ends, insecurities, surprises, fear, sadness, and celebration. Pam Ogden honestly and beautifully takes us on the journey with her. A real gift to anyone who has adopted a child, a companion to an adoptive parent in the process, and a tutor to anyone who loves the orphan or the family and is willing to embrace the fear and joy of adoption."

—Jeff Schulte,
Founder, Executive Director, TinManMinistries.org

"In *He Made Me Brave*, Pam courageously takes us on her adoption journey with her son Hudson. The intriguing overseas adoption pilgrimage gave me insight into what each family may potentially experience. This book is a precious personal window into adoption that every family who hopes to adopt will find intimate and insightful. I loved this book and recommend it."

—**Brian Howard,**
Chairman of the Board and U.S. West Network Director, Acts 29

"Beautifully written, vividly descriptive, and courageous, Pam's journal entries give front row seat to the real joys and hardships of her family's adoption journey. It was as if I were right there with Pam and Jason, sharing in their incredible adventure. This book is a gift to those who are either considering or have already adopted or fostered children. It is a delightfully encouraging read."

—**Patrick Bowler,**
Planter and Pastor of Valley Life Church, Lebanon, Oregon

"In this little book, Pam Ogden shares a side of adoption we seldom hear about. She gives us a glimpse into her family's story, with all the raw emotions involved in their journey. It's a quick and engaging read—buy it, read it, let your heart be warmed by the personal reflection of our Father's love in the sometimes heart-wrenching adoption process."

—**Steve Timmis,**
CEO, Acts 29

"What a journey! From an obscure campground in Oregon to the bustling streets of Seoul, South Korea, Pam Ogden colorfully journals her and her husband's emotional labyrinth, which required persistent teamwork and culminated in the homecoming of little Eun-wu (Hudson), strapped to his daddy's back. Thank you, Pam, for giving us a first-hand look into the difficulties and rewards of international adoption. All who read your musings will profit from the story of how God brought this sweet boy into your lives. May all who tread this same path find encouragement and hope from your experiences."

—**Steve McGuyre,**
Pastor of Valley Life Church, Lebanon, Oregon

He Made Me Brave

Embracing the Fear and Joy of Adoption

a memoir

For my very best
Japan Adoption friend – Amanda
I am extremely grateful
for you, and I hope
to someday write a

PAM OGDEN

second adoption
story book that ends
with the joyful day that
you and I introduce our
sweet Japanese babies to
each other!

Pam Ogden

LUCIDBOOKS

He Made Me Brave
Embracing the Fear and Joy of Adoption: A Memoir

Published by Lucid Books in Houston, TX
www.LucidBooksPublishing.com

ISBN-10: 1-63296-204-7
ISBN-13: 978-1-63296-204-1
eISBN-10: 1-63296-205-5
eISBN-13: 978-1-63296-205-8

Special Sales: Most Lucid Books titles are available in special quantity discounts. Custom imprinting or excerpting can also be done to fit special needs. Contact Lucid Books at Info@LucidBooksPublishing.com.

This book is dedicated to Hudson. You made my dreams come true; you gave me something to write about and something to fight for; you helped me to grow up, to trust God and to be humble; you gave me the chance to be strong and brave, and then tender and compassionate. I love you more than you can know. Thank you SO much for adopting me and for being my little boy. You're the best Hudson ever!

When I called out to you, you answered me.
You made me strong and brave.
Psalm 138:3 NIrV

TABLE OF CONTENTS

PREFACE

In 2012, we completed our first adoption and brought our 21-month-old son Hudson home from South Korea. During the trip to pick him up, I carried an iPad with me and journaled my thoughts. I didn't want to forget anything about this once-in-a-lifetime experience, and I needed something to distract me from the overwhelming anxiety I was feeling. I wrote the journal for myself. I didn't intend for it to be read by anyone else except, possibly, our son when he was old enough. I put all of my son's keepsakes away in the attic shortly after we returned home and forgot about the travel journal. When I finally opened it up to read through the memories and then flipped through the photos we took during the trip, I felt all those emotions again. They were sharp and sad and sweet and scary, and left me sobbing . . . which is why I hadn't looked at them for five years.

When we had decided to adopt Hudson, we started from zero—no knowledge of international adoption and no funds. But I felt a strange peace about it. I kept telling my husband, Jason, "I don't want to ask anyone for money. I have a feeling God is going to do something really cool, and I can't wait to see it." So while we informed friends and family about the adoption, we were careful not to ask anyone directly to help us with the costs.

Nevertheless, within five months, we raised $22,000. So many people rallied around us and supported us physically, prayerfully, emotionally, and financially, that we were absolutely awestruck. It was incredible. Through the grace of God, and with the help of our family and friends, we were able to make that first adoption a reality.

But we knew we wanted to adopt another child. We had said from the beginning, "If we adopt one child, we will adopt two children." We didn't want our child to feel different or as though they belonged any less than the others, so adopting from an Asian country the second time was a priority for us. We began looking into this second adoption, but because of the delays in almost every country, as well as the costs and the stress of the first adoption, we had difficulty following through.

One agency, Faith International Adoptions, appealed to us because they were able to match families with infants (as opposed to toddlers) from Japan. We contacted them repeatedly over the four years after we brought Hudson home. However, because they were such a small agency, they didn't have a waiting list and were not accepting new families. We gave up. We resigned ourselves to having five children and to trying to help our son feel loved and accepted among our biological kids.

Surprisingly, about a year after we stopped pursuing them, Faith International Adoptions e-mailed us and invited us to adopt another child. Jason showed me the e-mail, and we looked at each other for a tense moment. Finally, I told him, "Nah. We're too old. And that's a lot of money."

But the next day, the kids and I were out walking with some friends when my daughter Luka turned to me and said, "We could be carrying a little baby with us right now . . ."

It was a casual, innocent comment. She was holding my hand and enjoying the walk. She only said it because the thought struck her at just that moment.

But the idea stabbed me. Suddenly, I remembered four years of very specific prayers—prayers that I had given up on. I wasn't bitter about those unanswered prayers. I had just grown to accept that the answer was no. It was a selfish prayer anyway, born mostly of a desire to prolong the season of life that involved swaddling, kissing, feeding, and cuddling babies.

Mixed with the exhilaration I'd felt when we adopted Hudson, I also felt a consuming grief over the time I'd missed with him when he was an infant. At the risk of sounding overly dramatic, it felt as if I had brought home a child, but lost a baby. I grieved as if I had miscarried.

I had a baby. He was mine. I had held his picture in my hand, read the well-baby reports about his growth and development, and sent him care packages with Gerber Baby Puffs and a blue polka-dot Minky blanket. We had celebrated his first birthday with friends at a Korean restaurant and hung his photo from a balloon in the middle of the table because he was still in South Korea. But I had lost that baby. I can't type out how much that hurt.

I was ashamed of that grief. While all the wonderful people who had helped us bring him home congratulated us, celebrated with us, and smiled joyfully when they greeted us, I felt a guilty, secret sorrow I couldn't express.

I spent my days building a bond with my sweet new son, but at night I started praying for another baby. My prayers were embarrassingly detailed, and at first I wondered if it was wrong to even pray so specifically. But then I remembered my grandma telling me that God wants us to have the desires of our hearts, as long as they conform to his will.

So when Luka made that comment, I remembered those prayers and realized that the e-mail from Faith International Adoptions was EXACTLY what I had asked God for:

- I would bring home an infant. The babies adopted through this agency are typically between four and eight weeks old.
- We could adopt from Japan, so Hudson would have a sibling he could relate to on a level he couldn't with our other children.
- The agency had contacted us. The fact that we had given up didn't stop God from answering.

He hadn't said, "No." He had just said, "Not yet."

I felt a shiver of excitement, and I took out my phone to text Jason. What would I say? We had already agreed to turn down the offer, an offer that had taken five years to come to us.

I typed, "Maybe we should tell the adoption agency we are interested," and touched "send."

Jason's immediate answer was, "Serious?" He told me later that my previous quick refusal had disappointed him.

He started working on the application right away. The accompanying fee was $300. On the day that he finished it, we had exactly $300 to spend. He put the application and the check in an envelope, addressed it, and took a picture of it to record the day we started our second adoption.

He told me that just after he started the car to drive to the post office, the song "Kings and Queens" by Audio Adrenaline came on. The lyrics in the song are a call to remember and care for orphans.

Soon after, I started a blog to inform our friends and family of our fundraising events. I included excerpts from my travel journal to give some background on the second adoption. Those blog posts grew into this book, and that is why most of the chapters are very raw and honest journal entries.

I have two goals for this book. I want to show the realities of adopting a toddler because when we were adopting, most of the literature available was either instructional, or it contained a picture of adoption that was quite romanticized. We didn't find many books that gave a clear picture of what it would be like to bring home a child who had already bonded with foster parents, but who was too young to understand what was happening.

My second goal is to raise funds for a second adoption. We hope to bring home a sibling for Hudson. So thank you for purchasing this book. You are helping us to reach these goals.

"Hope deferred makes the heart sick, but a longing fulfilled is a tree of life."

—Proverbs 13:12 NIV

INTRODUCTION

When we told our five children that we were going to adopt another baby, our two oldest girls gasped and started squeal-begging us to make it happen, as if we didn't really mean it when we told them in the first place.

Our youngest daughter asked for details: "When would we get the baby? Where would the baby come from? Would it be a boy or a girl?"

Our older son didn't have much of a response; he must not have been paying attention. In fact, when we made the announcement to our neighbors later, he yelled happily, "Wait! You didn't tell me this!"

But our younger son's reaction was the most poignant.

Five years prior, we had brought him home from South Korea, where he had spent his first 21 months with kind, loving foster parents. Our family was matched with him when he was only 9 months old, but because of delays in the mechanics of adoption, we had to wait a full, agonizing year to actually meet him. Old enough to have formed vital bonds with family (foster/biological/or adoptive), but too young to understand the complicated process of adoption, he was at probably the most difficult age to make such a devastating transition.

From his perspective, he was torn from his "mommy" and "daddy," his secure home, and everything he knew. And we, despite our desperate longings to love and care for him, were the catalysts for that trauma.

The transition was a difficult one, and its effects were long lasting. I felt a need to protect him against any perceived bias toward my other children on a daily basis, and to prove to him that I loved him. From the day we met, he held me at a distance, regarding me almost suspiciously. Our

1

relationship was strained, and it wrecked me. I hoped and prayed that with time, he would grow to understand more, and things would improve, but life was often a quiet battle between us.

On this day, however, things changed.

After we had told the kids, I climbed up into the attic to retrieve the blue nylon tote bag that our adoption agency had provided on the day we met Hudson. They had placed his important documents and a few personal items from his foster family inside. Once we returned home, I had added the outfit he wore when we met him, his bottle, maps of Seoul and all of our souvenirs from the trip, and then zipped it closed and put it away. It was fun to pull everything out as a family, remembering and talking about each item. Then, reminded of the memories I had recorded on the iPad, I searched through my old computer files until I found the travel journal — the one I had written in obsessively, more for my own sanity and distraction than for sentimental reasons. I honestly hadn't read it since we had come home.

Shortly after we returned, I had created a hardbound memory book about the adoption with photos and text that Hudson memorized. But the travel journal was a perspective that he had never heard before. I took it to the living room and started reading it out loud to the kids. Several times, I had to pause because the memories were overwhelming. When we came to the description of our first meeting, Hudson slipped quietly out of the room. A few minutes later, we heard him crying piteously in his bedroom. I went in and held him and cried with him. I asked if he could tell me what made him so sad, and he said he missed Korea, and that it was a sad story.

It WAS a sad story.

I don't think he had ever thought about how sad it was for everyone involved. Hearing it read to him was painful. But healing.

I comforted him the best I knew how, holding him and allowing him to grieve. I reminded him that we'd stopped reading at the sad part, but that the story had happy parts, too. We talked about those happy parts: playing on a playground in Korea, eating at McDonald's on our first day together, flying home and being greeted by friends and family at the airport, the Welcome Home party at Oma and Opa's house, and having a new brother and three sisters to play with.

After a few minutes, he calmed down, the grief having been lanced like an abscess. Soon he was distracted by things in his room and the mood changed. I told him we didn't have to read anymore. We could do something else.

But less than twenty minutes later, he came to me and asked me to read him the rest of the story. Wrapping his arms around my waist, he told me I was the best mom ever. Then, he said something that hit me hard.

"Thank you for adopting me, Mommy. And thank you SO much for adopting another baby."

He was grateful to us! Of all the reactions I had anticipated, I had never expected him to thank us. I squeezed him close and thanked him for being my little boy.

Hudson is now a changed kid. When I talk to him, he hears me. He repeats those same words to me several times a day, seeking me out, hugging me tightly no matter where we are or who is watching.

"Thank you for adopting me. And thank you for adopting another baby."

He cannot wait to be a big brother. And he's going to be a great one.

SOME HISTORY

I had difficult pregnancies. I went into labor at around 25 weeks with all four babies. After countless hospital stays, medications, and weeks of bed rest, all four still came early, the earliest at 32 weeks. Fortunately, only one of my babies spent time in the NICU, and only one has had long-term complications because of prematurity. But the efforts to stop early labor took a toll on me, physically and emotionally, and ultimately the risks to the babies convinced us not to try for any more biological children.

Though we knew we wanted a large family, we didn't consider adoption at first. Instead, we grieved. Then, slowly, God worked on both of us. We had a "Really? You, too?" conversation one day, and it became clear that the idea had been growing in both of our hearts.

We jumped into the world of adoption almost blindly. In September of 2010, we filled out an application with an agency. Because of the need in Haiti at that time, we intended to adopt a child or a sibling group from there. But shortly after we started the process, Haiti's program shut down indefinitely. So we started looking into Ethiopia. Then that program slowed significantly. Our social worker suggested that we try South Korea, so we began raising funds, scheduling home studies and learning about the Korean program.

About one year later, in September of 2011, we were staying at my parents' house when our social worker called me. Recognizing the number, I took the phone out to the front yard, answered it, and plugged my other ear so I wouldn't miss anything. She asked me if we were sure that we were willing to adopt a toddler rather than an infant, as we had originally planned.

I said, "Yes," that we had talked about it and decided we were prepared to care for a toddler if there was one for us.

She said, "Well, that's great news. Because I have a match for you. I'm going to e-mail you his information right now."

I said, "Really? Are you serious?" far too many times, and then threw open the front door to make the announcement.

We had a baby.

My parents, Jason, and I crowded around my mom's laptop, giggling and pointing and crying at the photos of a sweet 9-month-old baby boy.

Who would belong to us.

Who was ours from the moment we called back and said the word, "Yes."

Who was meant to be ours even before that.

We had no idea on that day how long it would actually be before we could hold him. The adoption process slowed dramatically until it seemed to be grinding to a stop. The wait was maddening as new delays continued to pop up. Wait-times for parents anticipating travel increased from just a handful of months to a year or more.

We answered weekly, daily, sometimes hourly questions from caring and concerned friends about the status of our adoption, shrugging our shoulders and feeling twinges of resentment about the reminder of the delay. It felt cruel. We missed his first birthday, his first steps, his first word, his first Christmas. I grieved the loss of each day.

Almost exactly one year later, we had finally raised all of the funds, completed all the paperwork, prepared our kids and our home for another family member, and were just waiting . . . waiting for a travel call.

On Tuesday, August 28, 2012, the kids and I were camping with my parents, and we had taken the kids to play at the river. I was watching the time because I had to be at a Children's Ministry meeting at 7:00 that evening. At 6:20, one of the staff members texted me and asked if I was coming. She said they were all there waiting for me. I had obviously written down the wrong time. I considered whether or not I should still go because by the time I got there, they would have been waiting for an hour. She told me to come anyway, that they would work on other things until I arrived. I hated to leave the river. My children were playing happily in the water. It was such a peaceful, warm evening. I drove quickly and said a prayer that the trip would not be wasted.

I had little to add to the meeting. The staff passed around a photo of a friend's brand new, sweet baby boy, and I felt the tears threatening. Pastor Steve asked me how things were in the nursery, and I told him, honestly, how difficult it had been for me to hold all of the precious babies in there lately. I confessed tearfully that I'd been relieved to avoid it for a couple of months. Then the meeting came to a stop while everyone waited patiently for me to start breathing again.

We had waited a year since we said, "Yes, we want that baby boy," two years since we filled out our initial application, and still no travel call. We knew we were so close, but every day he was less of a baby and more connected to his world in Korea. And every day would make his transition to our family more difficult. I missed him terribly, and I'd never even met him.

The group prayed for me. They asked for a quick and smooth transition for our whole family.

And a phone call.

We closed our meeting, and I drove back to the campground, spent and a bit embarrassed.

The next morning, after we had cleaned up the campsite, we drove home. I walked in our front door and heard Jason's voice, "Are you ready to go to Korea?"

First a thrill, then fear, and then disappointment that I had missed the phone call.

"We leave in two days, and meet our son in a week."

LAST DAY

Thursday, August 30: This is our last day in the States. Yesterday I was camping with my kids and my parents. Tomorrow I'm going to Korea. This time in between is thrilling. Terrifying. Confusing.

My parents took Ivan and Ember to their house with them, so only the two older girls are here. They don't feel the same urgency as I do. We are still at home, so for them nothing has changed yet. Except that Mommy is very distracted. They play quietly together until they have a question. Then they search the house for me (I could be anywhere), present their request and wait patiently. It takes at least 90 seconds for me to actually HEAR their question because the roar of my inner dialogue is deafening. I have to force myself to attend to the mental echo of their voices. My thoughts sound like this:

(Subconsciously note that Kelly appears in the doorway of the kitchen.)

"These bananas are ripe, I better send them up to my parents' house so they don't go bad while we're gone. Oh, I'm by the medicine cabinet, I'll take Luka's medicine and put it in her suitcase. Swimsuits! I need to pack swimsuits for the kids. I wonder if I will need a swimsuit . . . will there be a pool where we are staying in Korea? Ugh, no, I can't even swim, who cares if there's a pool. If the plane crashes, I hope it crashes over the land and not the ocean because I can't swim. WHAT? Nobody's going to SWIM their way home from a plane crash. (Gory Titanic-like image of plane crash victims bobbing in the ocean.) STOP! Mental reset. Dear Jesus, please give me strength and peace . . . Feed the cat. Feed the cat a LOT. How many days until my in-laws get here? One . . . two . . . three . . . four . . . Change the sheets on our bed so they can sleep in there."

See Kelly looking at me expectantly. *What did she just ask me?*
Rewind memory. "Mommy, did you feed us breakfast yet?"

Have to keep grounding myself because I'm starting to wonder if this
is what the beginning of mental decline feels like. What am I doing right
now? I'm wearing my Korea shirt in celebration. Celebration of a plane
trip that just a few months ago terrified me so much that I was trying
desperately to get out of it. Would it be weird if my dad went with Jason
instead of me . . .? Yes. That would be weird. And I would regret it for
the rest of my life.

The weather website says that the temperature is the same in Korea today as it is here. Our boy is over there doing things. Living. Everyone is over there living, just like they do every day. Somehow that's comforting.

I'm packing Luka's suitcase . . . blue swimsuit because it matches her eyes. Will I see her again? Will this be the last day I spend with her?

I'm preparing for this trip like I'm preparing for a wedding. Tried to get my hair done just hours before we left. SO disappointed that I will have to experience this life-changing event with mousy, grown-out roots. Notice a hole under the waistband of my underwear. Well, I can't wear THAT to Korea . . .

I can hardly stand to leave my cat before we close and lock our front door. I hold her like she is another of my babies, afraid to leave the comfort of her. This is the last time we'll be in this house without Hudson.

Driving to my parents' house. Van bulging with obsessive-compulsively packed luggage. Both girls asleep in their car seats. Listening to a Laurie Berkner song about sailing away over the ocean. I'm going to miss it. I want to drink these children in and not forget how they look, sound, smell.

So many people have helped to make this all possible. I can't even count them all. I am so grateful and humbled. I feel less alone with my fears when I remember all the people who have supported us.

I'm going to be an international traveler. How strange is that? I will say things like, "When we were in Korea . . ." I will look back on the plane ride, and my memory of 14 hours will be condensed into a few minutes. I will forget parts of this trip. Even though I've anticipated it every day for two years, it will only happen once.

Hudson's foster mom is taking care of him on the other side of the planet right now. She knows he is about to be torn away. But he doesn't. He is eating, sleeping and playing in his "home." We are going to do something awful to him. To erase his entire world. A toddler's nightmare: to be separated from his "mommy." His well-baby check-up report said that he calls his foster parents the Korean words for "mommy" and "daddy." That broke my heart when I read it. But it shouldn't. How wonderful for him to have spent these first two years in the comfort and security of a loving family, rather than in an orphanage, waiting for strangers to come and rescue him from a place where he has not been loved.

We will be jettisoned in an arc over the earth. Isn't that a fantastic thought? While people are picking up dirty laundry, curled on a couch watching TV, filling their cars with gas, we will be in a timeless, temperature-controlled missile, attached to the world by nothing. With only a mattress of air under us. I am giddy with wonder and terror at this thought. I almost don't believe it. Like I will walk into the door of an airplane, and rather than ME moving, my surroundings will change while I am shut inside, and I will step out in awe 14 hours later.

TRAVEL DAY 1

Friday, August 31: Up at 1:00 a.m. Take three-year-old to the bathroom. She nods sleepily on the toilet. Limp in my arms, back to bed. She is oblivious. Content. I smile at her sleep noises.

Browse Facebook in the dark. Pinterest . . . too many recipes for my nervous tummy. This is the beginning of our travel day.

Kelly knew we were going to leave early this morning. She cried pitifully at bedtime last night. Pinching the skin on my arms, she was holding me so tight. I couldn't do anything to comfort her. When I went to bed, I left her sobbing on her sleeping bag surrounded by things to distract her: books, video games, toys. A raw reminder of what we are about to do to Hudson.

Leaving a personal letter and a box filled with daily gifts for each of our kids. I'm sad to miss their reactions.

Keep testing myself, "Fourteen hours ago, what was happening? Could I be on a plane for that long?"

Too quickly, it is time to go to the airport. We kiss our children's heads as they sleep. Ember wipes her cheek where Jason kissed her, never opening her eyes.

In the car on the way to the airport. Willing myself blindly forward, refusing to listen to my fears.

Leaving my dad at security. I can't help crying. We walk down the corridor toward our gate, which is parallel to the corridor my dad is following to leave the airport. Just when I am overcome with sobs, I see him waving to us from a window connecting the two corridors, and I laugh. I adore him.

At Starbucks. I'm not cool like these other air travelers with their iced coffees and Red Bulls. I have my Gatorade and Saltines. Jason is in line. A long line. He doesn't know how desperately I want him to come back. So that I'm not just standing here alone, guarding our bags while hundreds of unfamiliar faces sweep by.

Sitting at our gate. Listening to the sound of luggage wheels across the carpet and enjoying the SPACE around myself. Feel like I might poop or pee or vomit.

Hope I don't have to sit by that person.

Don't know how to just sit. How do people do that? Need to be moving, doing something, distracting myself. My hands are tingling. My eyes burn.

Boarding the plane to LAX. So tight. So crowded. The anxiety medication I took before I left the house is not enough. I swallow another.

Taking off. I am sweating, shaking, forced into submission by the fantastic lift of the plane. Sobbing. No one notices but Jason. They are preoccupied with their thoughts. This is like a ride on a city bus for them. They talk, laugh, read newspapers. I sit with my barely tolerable level of anxiety.

The woman in front of me is holding a little boy wrapped in a thick blanket. He was talking when we took off, but is now asleep in her lap. I ask her how old he is, and she says, "Two." The short interaction calms me.

Sun shining through the window on the other side of the plane. Feels like the world is tilting. The light moves across the walls as we turn.

Halfway there . . . counting minutes until we arrive. The lady in front of us is coughing and the lady next to us is sneezing.

Use the bathroom. Like a Porta Potty in the sky.

The seats look old. Chipped paint, dirty hinges, outdated designs. I worry for a minute that the passenger in front of me will be the last one that seat can hold, and he might end up in my lap. Which naturally makes me concerned for the quality of maintenance on the rest of the plane.

The pilot is announcing something quiet and garbled about our descent.

I am in the aisle seat, Jason is in the middle, and a woman is reading a book by the window. We are descending, and she comments on Jason's iPad. After noticing how soothing conversation is, I am hungry to talk to her. She is on her way to Peru to celebrate her 40th birthday with a friend. Jason tells her about our adoption.

Going down. Ears popping. Rush of air sounds different. We are almost to LAX. Oh, how I wish we were at our final destination already.

We land, and I feel like I have been holding my breath. I want to run off the plane.

I feel energized by my success on the first plane ride.

LAX is a confusing mass of people, all hurrying around an indoor city. We keep asking how to get to our terminal. We must exit the building completely and walk the entire length of the building outside, dodging travelers climbing in and out of cars with their luggage.

At one point, we pass a black Cadillac Escalade and suddenly a group of men with expensive cameras pushes past us to get close to it. A man steps out of the car, and a hand appears through the open door handing him something. We wonder who this celebrity is as we pass.

We enter another building for international flights and find the counter for Korean Air. The women behind the counter are beautiful, young, and slender. There is some confusion about whether or not we can purchase Hudson's return plane ticket now. A man at the counter tries to help us. He keeps saying we need to call and make a "rez-uh-ba-ton." We explain that we were told to buy the ticket now so that we can be sure there is enough room on the plane. After some conversation between him and one of the beautiful, soft-spoken ladies, we are able to purchase the ticket. When she hands it to Jason, he notices that the name is spelled wrong and shows it to her. She apologizes and makes a new one.

I am so thankful for my husband right now. It occurs to me that if he was not as clear-minded and confident as he is, we could never do this. He cannot draw on any strength from me. He is carrying me through this and is responsible for all the details and decisions. I am suddenly broken with appreciation. I follow him like a child.

Checked in, now waiting for our Korean Air flight. We are really heading toward our boy now. Hitting a wall of exhaustion already.

On the Korean airplane. Much bigger and nicer. The flight attendants are stunning. Blue silk tops tucked into white, knee-length skirts, white collar and white scarf. They hand us each a little packet with a toothbrush, toothpaste and some thin slippers that look like giant maxi pads.

There is an Asian family behind us with two little boys. They are quiet and calm.

Watching the movie *What to Expect When You're Expecting.* Headphones are way too big . . . keep sliding down to my neck. Two hours in, they serve us lunch: Korean bibimbap.

Reading letters sent with us from family and friends. I have enough to read one every hour. Such dear, wonderful things they have written to me.

The lights are turned off, and the window shades drawn so people can sleep. I see sunlight peeping through the cracks in the window shade, and it comforts me. We are following the sun.

Write out a letter to the foster mom. I don't know what I could possibly say to her that would be enough. I'm including a gift for her, and I'm hoping to receive photos from Hudson's first two years in return.

I have a giant travel zit on my cheek. Lovely for photos.

It's 6:00 p.m. in Oregon. My kiddos are probably finishing dinner and playing before bed.

The flight attendants walk up and down the aisles asking if we need anything. When they aren't busy, they sit in a seat attached to the back wall with their hands folded in their laps.

This morning already seems like days ago.

So many times today I have had to force myself not to listen to my fears and to just push on. I've had to make sacrifices and conquer fears for all of my babies, but this one feels the biggest. I am throwing off all my comfort and defenses and running straight into the face of my fear.

We are sitting behind the bathroom wall, so we hear the toilet flush over and over.

Me: "What was that?"

Jason: "Sounded like a phone dropping."

Me: "Was it mine . . .?"

Jason: "Yours is in your hand."

Only two more hours until we reach Tokyo. Starting to feel relieved.

I use the bathroom, and on my way out, I try to open the accordion door with a paper towel in my hand, but the paper towel is slippery, and the door slams shut. A flight attendant is standing just outside the door. She must think I can't get out, so she opens it for me. Silly American.

Turbulence. Feel like I'm in a boat. Once, there is a quick drop and then a sharp rise, and all over the cabin I hear exclamations of surprise. We are only one hour from Tokyo now. Exhausted.

We are descending! Just over Tokyo. Our eyes are burning, our bodies ache. Almost there. Two-hour stop in Tokyo and then on to Korea.

Strange how similar this experience is to birth: the lonely wakeful night, laced with adrenaline and anticipation. Nausea and hunger commingled. Doubt about my adequacy as Mommy.

Finally, we've landed. We're on the other side of the world!

At the Tokyo airport. When we get off the plane, we have to take all of our things, exit the plane with the other passengers, follow them up the escalator, down the hall, through immigration, down another hall, through security, and then back down an escalator and through the building to the waiting area right next to the gate we just left.

Everyone here speaks quietly, like in a library. Muzak is piped in . . . George Michael "Never Gonna Dance Again."

The Asian family that rode behind us on the last flight is sitting across from us. Their children were so quiet on the flight, I forgot they were there.

Jason comes out of the men's restroom. He says that while he was in there, a female janitor came in and refilled the toilet paper.

Barely conscious as we board our last flight, I try to sleep once we take off, but can't get comfortable.

One hour left of our last flight. I don't feel funny anymore. Don't feel like joking. I'm sweaty and sore and crabby and tired. Longing for a place to lie down. After we get through customs and baggage claim, we still have a van ride.

Lots of dozing and heads nodding on this flight. A little girl is singing, and I keep dreaming that it's my Ember.

Landing in Seoul. Hallelujah. Praise God who created us to travel on the GROUND.

We have to sit in the plane for a while because our gate is being used. Then we follow the directions the adoption agency sent us through immigration, baggage claim, and customs to find our van driver, a muscular young man in a tank top and shorts. He's an aggressive driver. Feel like we are living a role-playing game.

"It's 40 minutes ride," he says. He doesn't try to make conversation with us, which is fine. I am too tired to think.

Feel like I'm on another planet. Dark and foggy, but so many lights. The speedometer is in km/hr. The red line is on 140.

Jerking along, bumper to bumper. Either the Dramamine® is still working, or I'm too tired to be carsick.

We arrive at the guest house down tiny, zigzagging alleyways barely wide enough for the van to pass through.

Inside is a playroom fenced by couches. A slender, older man greets us from behind a reception desk at the back.

"You taka off you shoes, see?" He opens a cupboard with several pairs of thin, worn slippers inside, then points at our shoes and then at the slippers several times, chuckling. Then he points out a hook at the desk with

our room key on it. Outside the door, he shows us a keypad, and says, "Personal code . . . personal code." He shows us which buttons to push to open the door. I am hoping Jason is paying attention because my senses are shot.

Our host leads us to an elevator that would send anyone with an elevator fear into a panic. Slowly, slowly the car ascends, stops, then pauses maddeningly before the doors slide open. Jason and the host step out of the elevator onto the fifth floor. I pull my suitcase toward the door but it closes before I can get out.

Seriously.

I scan the metal buttons . . . looking for the one that opens the door. None of them look right to me. A few agonizing seconds later, the door opens and Jason is standing there looking at me quizzically. Thank you for saving me, oh Brave Husband.

TRAVEL DAY 2

Sunday, September 2: (We lost Saturday, September 1 when we crossed the International Date Line.) We sleep until 4:00 a.m. We both turn over and look at each other. It's about lunchtime at home, so we dress and get ready for the day.

Leave our room, feel like we walk into a wall of steam, scuff down the hall in our strange slippers, and discover that the elevator is turned off for the night, so we use the stairs. Feels like we're sneaking. All is dark except for the signs marking each floor. Down to the lobby. Hang our room key on the hook at the desk, trade our slippers for shoes.

Then Jason uses the flashlight app on his phone to figure out how to open the sliding glass door. He steps outside, and I wait to see if he can use the "personal code" to get back in. He pushes the buttons and the door slides open with a sound that reminds me of a Star Trek movie.

Outside, I have to tie my sweatshirt around my waist because it is SO HOT, even at 5:00 a.m. Jason has his backpack and a handful of won. We wander down the street past a couple sitting at a metal table covered with dishes and green bottles. They don't acknowledge us.

The air smells different here. Like hot metal, sea water, and sewer.

At the end of the block is a 7-Eleven. Relieved to find something we know, we walk in. Pop music with English lyrics is playing. Packages look familiar but all the logos are in Hangul. I recognize a few things: Oreos, Lay's Potato Chips. Find the refrigerated section and scan labels helplessly until I see a small bottle that says "Real Yogurt" with a picture of a mango. Pick that up. We buy three bottles of water because the information we received said not to drink the tap water. Jason buys a coffee drink and two rolls of sushi. I also pick up a cup of Jell-O® with fruit suspended in it, a styrofoam bowl of what appears to be ramen, and a vacuum pack of little sausages. We set our things on the counter, and a teenage boy scans them all and announces our total. Jason and I look at him blankly. He points to the little screen beside the counter, which says 15,200 won. Jason counts out the bills and gives them to him. Then the cashier puts all our purchases in a plastic bag and tosses a few wooden chopsticks in paper sleeves on top. Proud of our success, we make our way back to our room. The sushi is good, and the yogurt soothes the gnawing in my tummy.

Our room is small and L-shaped. When you walk in the door, there is a tiny entry and then a step up onto the "ondol," a heated floor, which covers the rest of the room. We both trip on it several times before we get used to it. It's nice to have warm feet, though. Especially since the air-conditioner is always on.

There is a twin bed and a full bed against one wall, both with hard mattresses, blankets, and one flat sheet that feels like canvas.

Two of the four walls are floor-to-ceiling windows with tattered vertical blinds running the length of them. There is a crib with blankets, and a table and chairs that look like they belong on a patio.

About a foot above the floor, a metal box housing an American-style outlet is plugged into the wall. When you flip the switch, it makes a sharp humming sound.

The whole bathroom is a shower. When you turn the knob, water splashes on everything: the toilet, the garbage can, the toilet paper, and anything you've naively set on the floor. Like your pajamas and underwear.

The computer is in the hallway, backed up to huge windows that look out on the neighborhood. The buildings are so close together, it doesn't look like there is room for streets in between them. Trees grow right on the flat roofs. The building residents apparently consider the roof another room. There is laundry hung across one, a mattress propped up on another, and a man leaning over the wall smoking on a third.

We are watching TV, and a commercial comes on. A young man is cheerfully preparing breakfast, cracking eggs in a dish, stirring with a spoon.

22

The narration is in Korean, but the background jingle sounds familiar. It is a woman singing in English with a Korean accent. She sings, "Oh happy day . . . oh happy da-a-ay . . . when cheh-suh wah . . ." and then the lyrics start over. I finally identify it as a fragment of the first line of an American gospel hit.

We watch a show that is narrated in Korean but seems to be a version of MTV's *Real World* for dogs. The set includes a sign that says "Dog's" above the silhouette of a dog pooping.

Today, our adoption agency has arranged and paid for a tour of Seoul, guided by a college student who is working on her English. We are so grateful and excited to see the culture and the city, but we are fighting fatigue.

We go downstairs to meet our tour guide. She is sitting on a bench in the lobby writing in a spiral notebook. The lobby attendant motions her over to us. Petite, beautiful skin, glitter on her eyelids, charm bracelets on both arms, pale blue lacy top and jean shorts, orange tennis shoes and mustard colored ankle socks, hair pinned back with a large bow. Leather backpack with the English word "philosophy" printed on it.

She shows us her notebook and says, "I have prepare something for you . . ." Then she turns her notebook horizontally and flips the pages as she reads what she has written, each page in a different color marker. She introduces herself as "Juhee" and says she is very happy to meet us, and that she hopes we will have happy memories, but she asks that we would be patient with her because her English is not perfect. Later, she tells me the idea came from the movie *Love Actually* where the man proposes that way.

We walk down the street toward the subway. Each time I walk outside, I am struck by the humidity. Like I have walked into a giant mouth. The air around me is like a hot tongue.

On the subway, Juhee says her English name is "Flower," and that she thinks it is a very impressive name. She is irresistibly kind and friendly.

The subway system is huge! She tells us that from 8:00 to 9:00 a.m. and from 6:00 to 7:00 p.m. the subway is so full that the handrails are unnecessary because the crowds of commuters stand shoulder to shoulder, holding each other up.

Riding, riding again. Seems like we are forever riding in some kind of vehicle.

"Annyong haseyo" is hello.

"Kamsa hamnida" is thank you.

She compliments us on our pronunciation.

We show her our picture of Hudson and she says, "Cute! I love big eyes because I have small eyes." She smiles her adorable smile. She is like pure sunshine.

She tells us, "We think adopting is happy work. But we don't do it. It's very sad things. We must change."

She tells us that "gwiyeopda" means "cute" and that we should say that when we meet Hudson because it will make the Korean ladies smile.

We step off our subway and board another one. Jason almost misses the doors closing once. I feel a little better about being trapped in the elevator.

I don't understand how people don't fall down in the subway cars. The other riders stand easily while looking at their phone screens as the car jerks forward and tilts side to side. I am gripping the handrails like an inexperienced sailor.

We are headed to Gyeongbokgung Palace, which Juhee pronounces "Puh-LACE." It is incredible. Built in the 14th century, destroyed by fire, abandoned, and then gradually restored to its original glory. Sprawling buildings and pavilions painted with rich, vivid colors, and surrounded by delicate trees and a peaceful lotus pond.

Juhee says that when she was in elementary school, her class came here, and "it was very boring. But now it is interesting."

I try to stop saying "Wow!" all the time, but it is the best way that I can express my awe and wonderment. Juhee exclaims, "omygah!"

When we look at the traditional hanboks sewn with gold thread, she says, "Koreans love gord. Koreans wear hanbok at New Year's Day."

We stop at an enormous fabric scroll. "I don't understand how can read this . . . so big!" she says with her arms spread wide. I love her! I want to take her home with me, too!

She beckons us with a clawing motion, fingers pointing downward, and when she has a question, she runs with her arms out from her sides to ask the nearest stranger.

A glass display box holds huge hair pins that look like daggers.

In the courtyard, the dirt is like grit under our shoes. Everywhere we go, the sidewalks are made of bricks of varying shapes fit together in mosaic patterns.

Crowds of people shove to see inside a window of the palace. Koreans have a very different sense of personal space. They bump and jostle each other constantly, but it is not considered disrespectful at all. We wait patiently for our turn to peer inside a window, but no space ever opens up. Juhee takes my wrists and pulls me up to take her place, so I can see.

The massive stone stairs are made of blocks of granite. She shows me the word "granite" on her phone screen.

The men wear what we would consider Capri pants here, and many of them smoke.

We hear an extremely loud cicada in a tree. I thought I had heard a cicada before but never one this loud. It sounds like machinery.

I tear up every time I see a baby. They are so beautiful, and I get to take one home.

A group of children run down the stairs. They are wearing matching red shirts, evidently on a school field trip. Juhee translates their shouts for us, "It's so boring. Let's go home!"

We are all hungry after walking around the palace. Juhee asks us what we like to eat. We list all kinds of food. When we mention Japanese food, she says, "Japanese food is very small! I eat all of food but I'm still hungry!" She tells us repeatedly that she LOVES American food.

We take the subway to Insadong. It is quaint and cheery, full of tiny alleys with brick paths, mazes of narrow channels and tiny shops. I keep tripping on the uneven stones, which is embarrassing until I notice other people tripping, too.

There are information guides wearing red uniforms, standing on corners everywhere, waiting to help.

Juhee takes us to a tiny doorway with narrow stairs that lead to a restaurant below ground level. We sit, and the waitress brings little moist washcloths sealed in plastic to wash our hands.

We each order a different dish, but it soon becomes clear that each item is meant to be shared with the group, rather than eaten individually. Juhee reaches across the table and mixes my food for me. She senses our inexperience at just the right moments and assists without even a hint of scorn, chatting happily the whole time.

So many little dishes of beautiful, colorful food. Everything is spicy. My nose is running. My lips are burning. She feeds us samples of each dish with her own chopsticks explaining and naming them all. So many tiny bowls of appetizers. Bulgogi, rice and barley with vegetables, and doenjang-jjigae soup.

Now I am full and sleepy. But there is more to see today.

We descend into the subway station again, but instead of riding, we find our way out one of the many other exits for this station. Now we are near Bukchon Hanok Village, a traditional Korean neighborhood full of beautiful old homes on very narrow winding streets and steep hills. Almost get run over several times. On the ground, there are metal markers that say, "photo stop." Places that are recommended for taking pictures. We stop at several and Juhee is our photographer.

She takes us to a Korean souvenir shop, where she has arranged for us to try some traditional Korean art. A tiny, crowded store with little stools at a work table. The woman inside is wearing a bright pink polo shirt. She leans over me and mumbles instructions in Korean and pushes my hands to guide them. We cover a plate and a luggage tag with hanji Korean paper. I am nervous because she is standing over us the whole time, monitoring how much glue we apply, which direction we brush it on, and how we tear the edges of the paper. When it is finished Juhee tells Jason that he needs to let it "freeze" for a little while.

We cross the street right in the middle of traffic.

At a coffee shop that is very Western-style, Juhee says, "We want to resemble American culture, especially coffee."

She asks Jason which is better: this coffee or Starbucks. Jason says emphatically, "THIS coffee." It is expensive though. About $5 for the "coffee of the day."

We continue in a loop around the village. All traditional houses with sloping tile roofs. There are persimmon trees heavy with fruit wedged up against the houses. Signs are posted reminding tourists that people actually live in these historic houses, and to be courteous and quiet. How strange to live in this prestigious old neighborhood, and have crowds of tourists flocking past your door every day. I spot an open door and peer inside, slippers left on a mat in an entry, a quaint courtyard garden.

Juhee asks us if we would like to try a traditional Korean beverage. We nod, "yes," so she finds a stand selling plastic cups of a cloudy liquid with bloated white bits at the bottom. "Sikhye" she pronounces for us. She explains that Koreans drink it on New Year's Day with rice cakes. She shoves three straws into the lid, and we all taste it. It is slightly sweet, with chewy pieces that arrive unexpectedly through the straw.

Juhee holds the cup up and points to it. "These white thing at bottom . . .?" She pauses for me to note them. I watch her mouth as she says, "Are LICE."

"Hmmm?" I say through a chewy mouthful with my eyebrows raised. She mistakes my surprise for misunderstanding, checks herself, and tries again, saying, "RICE." Jason says later that when she said "lice," he thought, *Well, it's pretty good lice. I guess I'll eat it.*

There are just as many men carrying babies here, even in front packs, as there are women. I never notice people as much in America as I do here. I can't help but study them. They are beautiful, and the babies are gorgeous.

We head back to the subway for our trip back to the guest house. Juhee finds us on Facebook and sends us each a friend request.

Everyone in this city carries a phone or a tablet. A woman sits down next to me on the subway. She appears to be older than me, but her phone case is a large three-dimensional yellow silicone teddy bear.

We stop in front of the Holt building. Juhee runs up to a complete stranger, an Asian young man walking with headphones on, and asks him to take our picture. Surprisingly, he speaks fluent English without even a hint of a Korean accent. He takes several pictures for us, some with our camera and some with her phone. When we thank him, he says, "My pleasure. Have a great day, you guys."

As he walks away, Juhee turns to me and says, "He has very good English! Is he Korean?"

At the guest house. I ask her to wait for a minute while I run upstairs and get her "Thank You" gift. Forget to take off my shoes until I am coming back downstairs. Embarrassed, I slip them off and shove them under my arm, continuing down the stairs in my socks. I hand her a gift bag full of goodies, and she says, "Thank you! And I have prepared something, too!" She pulls out a tiny envelope and two purses that she bought at the craft store. She says, "I never forget today," and smiles with her eyes almost closed. She is so pretty.

Back to our air-conditioned room. Want to crawl into bed. It's about 1:30 a.m. at home right now. Jason is going to 7-Eleven to get us some dinner.

Ahhh. Sitting in bed, we eat sushi and watch Korean game shows.

TRAVEL DAYS 3 AND 4

Monday, September 3: Wake up at 1:00 a.m. Can't sleep anymore. Read over my notes from the trip so far.

We have this day to ourselves with no agenda, so we decide to venture out on our own to Namdaemun Market. Attempt the subway again on our own. I am so proud of us!

Namdaemun is like the Portland Saturday Market on steroids. I don't think I can accurately express the sheer quantity of stimuli assaulting us here. The noise, the colors, the masses of merchandise piled everywhere, the snaking narrow paths. There are about 30 multi-level buildings, and endless street vendors between them. If we stop near one, the owner comes out and tries to convince us to buy anything from jewelry to socks, cell phone accessories, toys, figs, or pig knuckles.

We buy gifts for our kids at a store called Alpha that just keeps going up another floor and up another floor. Sprawling rooms and departments carrying cleaning supplies, art supplies, tools, toys, dishes . . . and on and on.

Outside, we merge into the crowd again. Pedestrians and traffic share space. I tell Jason that if I don't get run over by a motorcycle or a car while we're here, it will be a miracle. A few minutes later a man riding a motorcycle literally bumps into Jason.

We venture down a tight underground alley lined with tiny restaurants and are looking at the sample meals outside. Many of them have plastic representations of their dishes on a table outside the door. It is difficult to hear each other over the sounds of food preparation. A woman makes a square shape in the air with her fingers and yells "pict chah!" at us. We

don't understand. I show her the Korean word for the soup I had yesterday on my phone, and she shakes her head "no."

We walk a few more feet and another woman comes out of her restaurant and says "pict chah menu . . . English!" Then we understand. I show her the Korean word for the soup, and she says "Ah!" and eagerly waves us in. We start to walk through the door, and a woman inside shoves two menus in my hand, grips my wrist and literally pulls me to a table. We order bibimbop and soybean paste soup. The food is vibrant and full of flavor, brought to us in little cast iron pots so hot that the soup inside is still boiling.

This restaurant is brightly lit and very casual. Other customers chat and eat together, relaxed and absorbed in conversation. A Korean woman across from us is sitting in a booth with one stocking foot up on the seat next to her.

We emerge from the alley, out to the rows and rows of booths again. Two men are arguing in Korean near one of the booths. One of them pushes

the other. A third man steps between them and holds them apart. I want to shrink back into the crowd, but Jason is interested. He watches. Eventually one man walks away, and the other man sits on a stool outside of what must be his booth. It is full of jeans, piled up against every wall.

We find a large building that says "Children's Clothing" and walk in. It is crammed full of individual stalls of children's clothes, each run by a separate salesperson. The aisles are barely wide enough to walk through; I brush against piles of clothing with my purse on one side and my elbow on the other. It is very busy. We plan to come back and bring Hudson with us in a few days.

Just outside, a man is selling Asian pears the size of small melons. They are $5 apiece. Further down there is a man selling giant peaches two for $5. We buy them and tuck them in my bag to enjoy later.

We find gifts for everyone, and are finally tired of walking. It is difficult to find our way back to the subway. The aisles between stalls are not straight, and the market is immense.

The ride home builds our confidence as we prove that we have figured out how to get around the city on the subway.

A woman who was sitting when we enter gets up and stands uncomfortably close to me. Then she casually turns her phone screen toward me as she reads it. The text is in English. I understand, she wants me to notice that she can read English.

As we get off the subway we find a neighborhood map to decide which exit to take to get back to street level. When we are satisfied that we have chosen the right one, we follow the signs out and discover that we are on the wrong side of a VERY busy highway. Rather than cross, we return to the subway station and try another exit. I feel like Alice in Wonderland as we find that we are again on the wrong side of the highway. Crowds of students in uniforms are waiting to cross, so we decide to join them. They are happily visiting and laughing as we follow them past the traffic.

Home again. Jason heads back out to find dinner, and I lie down. We have decided that we should try to stay up until 7:00 or 8:00 so that we will sleep until later in the morning. But it is too hard. Even with the TV on, my eyes are crossing. Jason comes back, and we are both down for the night around 5:30.

Tuesday, September 4: Up at 1:00 a.m. again. Try to relax until 7:30, then head out to find Wi-Fi so we can Skype my parents and the kids. So wonderful to see their faces! We sit on the curb outside a building that has Wi-Fi, so it is difficult to hear when cars drive by.

We find a coffee shop called Able Coffee that has free Wi-Fi. Jason orders an Ethiopian coffee, and I have a kiwi smoothie.

We are able to iMessage friends back in the States. Now sitting here waiting for the downpour to stop. Here we are, Oregonians, caught without umbrellas!

The barista at the coffee shop offers us his umbrella. "I have two," he says. We promise to bring it back later.

Back to the subway, on our way to nearby shopping areas, Itaewon and then Dongdaemun. Itaewon is definitely geared toward Westerners. The salespeople speak English, and there are Korean tourist souvenirs. We even eat at Burger King. A hamburger is about $8. But the tomato slices are so red and ripe, it is worth the higher price.

The crosswalks here are twice as wide as at home, and there are arrows to show you which side of the crosswalk is intended for which direction. There are lighted symbols of people walking in green or stopping in red, and they come on automatically.

The rain is so heavy that we are splashing through standing water, and my canvas shoes are very uncomfortable. We stop in a Foot Locker, and I buy some flip-flops and squeak down the street and back into the subway.

We try walking around Dongdaemun, but it is too overwhelming. Huge stores and crowds of people. So many cosmetic shops. One called "Skin Food," and another called "It's Skin." Down the side streets are hundreds of stores each the size of a bathroom, with one employee inside managing his wares or service. We head back toward the guest house making our own video of "How to Use the Seoul Metro" on the way. While we are in the subway, we walk through the underground market. Endless corridors of tiny shops with fluorescent lighting.

Then back to Able Coffee to return the umbrella. The barista here speaks to us in English about our visit to Seoul. He says Itaewon "has good night life," and makes a drinking motion. "I like it," he says.

Plan to rest tomorrow before our big meeting. I feel both fascinated and warm toward this country and also long for home. Sometimes I forget that we are in another country, and I realize with a start, "We are in Korea!" and feel a thrill all over again.

Thunderstorm. Wow. Thunder that rolls and rolls and rattles the building, and rain so loud we can't hear the TV. The lightning is bright up here on the fifth floor.

I am eating ramen that looked safe in the convenience store but my lips are on fire.

Today was our last day alone. Tomorrow we meet our boy.

FAMILY DAY

September 5, Wednesday: Midnight. Wake to the sound of a group of men yelling outside. They have been getting louder and louder. They must be drunk. Singing, laughing and yelling for the past hour.

In 15 hours, we get our boy. Before we went to bed, we were talking about it. What will we do with him for the next two days? I only brought enough toys for a plane ride. Jason says, "I just realized, he's gonna have to eat! What will we feed him?"

Back at home, kids are starting back to school today. I am so thankful that we homeschool. We would be missing three of our children's first day of school, and Ivan's first day of kindergarten.

That fire ramen I ate before bed is not agreeing with me. I consider wrapping up in some blankets on the bathroom/shower floor for the rest of the night. I am amazed that people here can eat hot spicy food for every meal. The children must get used to it while they are very young.

I stand on my bed to look out the window. I see the men outside. One of them is stumbling so badly that his friends have him by the arms. He vomits in the street and starts to walk away, but his flip-flops fall off, and one of them is lying next to the other facing the wrong way. The man is bent double, hanging on to his friends, trying in vain to put his feet into the shoes. Finally he gives up and continues down the street barefoot.

A woman comes out with a broom and a pan of water and tries to rinse the vomit into a drain. She picks up the shoes and takes them inside the building. I lie back down thinking the men are gone, and I can sleep, but I hear them moving up and down the streets yelling and laughing hysterically. Maybe they are looking for the shoes.

4:00 a.m. Wind and rain. Hollywood quality at times. It is never completely dark here. The city lights keep the sky at predawn all night. Eleven hours left.

Jason sits up and says, "I keep waking up and thinking of random things. Do we have any wipes?" That's why I love him.

Watching TV. There are so many infomercials. Most of them are about products that help you prepare fish. When we are flipping through channels, we usually stop at anything in English, which means we have watched a lot of *Police Women of Maricopa County* and *Real Housewives of Beverly Hills*. Two thoughts: WHY are Korean people interested in this? And, good grief, THESE shows are representing American culture for us.

Now, we are watching a channel called Life for Woman. A Korean drama comes on, and Jason picks up the remote and says, "I've already seen this one . . . "

I check Facebook, eager to post the countdown in HOURS, instead of days, and find that my friends are already doing it for me! So many wonderful posts and comments! I want to save them all.

We think there is another couple in the room next door now. They have changed the sign-in screen on the computer to French. I would love to meet them.

Jason says, "Hudson's bags are packed. He has no idea what's going on." Poor little guy. He will probably be waking up soon from his very last night in the only home he's ever known.

I am looking through the Korean phrase book and find the word for "guest house." I tell Jason that it is "minbakchip," and he says confidently, "We're staying at the minbakchip," which makes me laugh. We are silly with anticipation and nerves this morning.

Jason is at the coffee shop, and I am cleaning up the room and getting ready for our appointment. I wonder if anyone ever feels prepared for this.

Jason is back. We are thinking we should go over to the office at the Holt building and make sure that's where we are supposed to go for our family meeting. Jason says, "Should I dress up? Should I shave? I'm nervous!" SO glad I'm not the only one.

We dress up and walk to the Holt building. It is a very modern sky-scraper. We walk off the fancy elevator and see a glass wall running the entire length of the hall. At first, we can't figure out how to get in. Then, we see a tiny panel attached to one of the glass frames that has the word

"push" engraved into it. Jason pushes it, and a whole glass panel slides away. We step into the office. A few ladies are sitting at desks, and they answer our questions in very quiet voices.

We are back in our room now. These are the last few quiet hours. There isn't much time, so we are going for a little walk and then we'll look for some lunch.

Back from our walk. Saw more city. More tiny shops, more fancy sidewalks, more motorcycles, more deafening cicadas. Jason leaves to find some lunch, and I am resting. Getting SO nervous.

1:15 p.m. Okay, I'm not nervous, I'm terrified. Clammy and shivering. What if the foster mom is already there, and we don't get to video the moment we meet? What if they won't let us video? What if I pass out and die of anxiety during the family meeting?

The walk to the Holt building entrance is like walking onstage. I'm weak and trembly with anticipation. When we finally arrive, DJ You, our agency's international adoption social worker, is outside, escorting another family to their car with their new son and the foster parents. The foster mom is crying but smiling. Her husband puts his arm around her as the family drives away in a taxi. We see only this short interaction, but it is touching enough to make me cry.

Then, DJ asks us to come upstairs with her. We ride the elevator, and she asks us a few questions about our trip so far. When we get to the office she says, "Well, it looks like your son is already here . . ." which makes my stomach flop.

She walks to a door marked "Meeting Room" and sticks her head in. She talks to someone for a minute, and then she walks back to us and says with a smile, "They have brought a large foster group . . . foster mom, foster auntie, and two foster sisters." Jason and I laugh. We ask if we can video and she says, "Yes, if you want to."

Then, she walks toward the door and calls us to come with her. As we walk in, I see several women sitting on a couch, and DJ is saying softly, "Oonoo-eh, Oonoo-eh."

Then, I see him.

Standing with his back against the coffee table looking expectantly at all the women. I recognize him from his pictures. Serious face. Fine hair. Plump upper lip. Wide, confident stance.

He has little interest in us. He is playing with a light-up toy that has been provided in the room. His foster mom speaks to him in Korean, gesturing to us and encouraging him. Slowly he bows to us. They have taught him the traditional greeting and want him to perform it for us.

DJ asks us to sit down on the other couch. We watch this little boy, our son, interacting with the women in his foster family for several minutes. He is no bigger than I expected him to be, but he is so busy! From one toy to the next, from one person to the next, never stopping.

I pull some toys out of my diaper bag, and he looks at them for a few seconds. Then I pull out a can of Gerber Puffs, and he comes right over to me to investigate. I pour a few in my hand and he takes them all in his fist and walks back to his foster family. He does this over and over, and soon he is taking them from me and feeding them to the other ladies.

I feel unsure of my role. He still seems very much like someone else's child. I am afraid to scare him by being too forward, and nervous to interact with him in a way that the foster family will think is strange or wrong.

DJ asks us if we have any questions for the foster mom. There is some confusion while we figure out how we will video and read questions and type answers all at the same time. With shaking hands, I pull out the iPad, embarrassed about my hesitance, my inadequacy at entertaining him, the confusion . . .

We start asking our prepared questions. DJ translates them, and his foster mom answers, and we try to type her answers as fast as they are translated. Meanwhile, Eun-wu (Oo-noo, as we find out his Korean name is pronounced) is making rounds between all of the ladies, playing with cell phones, feeding them puffs.

While asking our questions, it becomes clear that this little boy has been loved completely, with very little boundaries. He has been a little gem in this family. Cherished and spoiled. He is affectionate with the women, walking between them, touching them all. And they all obviously love him dearly. When we ask his foster mom what she would like us to tell him about her, she tears up and cannot speak. DJ says, "I think she is emotional." Eventually, her answer is, "Tell him that I love him." Jason and I are crying now too. This little boy, our son, sees his foster mother crying and walks over to her. He stands in front of her and stares at her with concern. Then he touches her face and hugs her. He doesn't know why she's crying. Which just kills me.

Too soon our list of questions is finished. DJ hands us a blue tote bag with a few of his items inside, a packet for immigration when we reach the States, and his medical file for our pediatrician.

This blue bag is all he is bringing to his new life.

I awkwardly present our gift for his foster mom, and then DJ says that we need to go down and have his last medical check. Everyone stands and walks to the elevator and the tension is sickening.

The exam is over in a few minutes, and our whole group is standing in the doctor's office looking bewildered. And then DJ says, "It's time to say goodbye." I can't believe how terribly sad this makes me.

It's over? Already? Now what do we do?

I try to give his foster mom a hug, but she is trying to hand Eun-wu to me, and he is reaching back for her. Finally, DJ ushers us all outside and tells us that we can take him to the guest house to play. I am confused. Is everyone coming? Do we take him now?

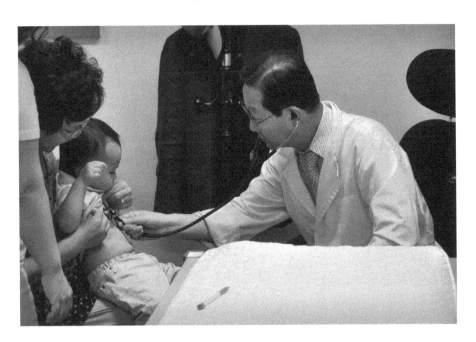

Family Day

One of the sisters is walking him up to the sidewalk so I follow. He is holding her hand. I reach down and take his other hand, which he takes willingly, and as we continue down the sidewalk, his sister lets go and backs away. When I look back, they are all standing at the door watching. We continue down the sidewalk until he trips, and I scoop him up, really holding him for the first time.

I am so confused, and nervous, and happy. We walk all the way to the guest house and take him up the elevator. He watches everything silently. Into our room. Close the door. A look of fear appears on his face. He whimpers. When I sit down, he pulls my hand trying to get me to stand back up. His whimpers become cries, and then wails of fear and confusion. Nothing will distract him. I am crying with him.

Everything we take out of his bag, he promptly puts back in, trying to rewind time to when we were still with his foster family. He pulls, pushes, shoves me toward the door, crying pitifully. He even picks up my slippers off the floor and tries to hand them to me. Our hearts are broken for him. I try to soothe him, carry him, rub his back, talk to him, but he will have none of it.

49

After half an hour of unsuccessfully trying to distract him, we decide to put him in the backpack carrier and take him for a walk. He is wary of Jason, so we put him on my back and head outside. This calms him. Occasionally I still hear him inhale sharply, the remains of hyperventilating.

We walk and walk and walk all over the neighborhood, and he is silent. When we walk past the coffee shop, the barista smiles at us through the window, waves and gives us two thumbs up. We stop at a grocery store and buy some milk for him. He is still quiet. I watch people's reactions. Because he is calm, I am a bit more relaxed. It comforts me that people have no idea that he is so new to us.

We walk a bit more, grateful that this is soothing to him, but aware that the distraction is temporary. We decide to take him to McDonald's. While Jason is ordering, two teenage girls come up and talk to him in the carrier. Then they ask me something in Korean. I look at them blankly, not sure how to respond, and one of the girls says, "Ahhhhh . . . where are

you from?" I answer, "The United States." They play with him, talk to him, shake his hand, and he bows his head to them.

We go upstairs to eat, and I am apprehensive about taking him out of the carrier. Will he try to run away? Will he scream and cry? We find a table and Jason lifts him out. He sits agreeably in his own chair next to mine. When I hand him a french fry, he takes it happily. He is content to sit and eat french fries and pieces of our sandwiches, and then he points to my Sprite. I hold the cup for him and he sips, and then turns his head away with his mouth open, surprised by the bubbles. Then reaches for the cup again. We eat our whole meal in peace. Our little boy enjoying the french fries and the soda, swinging his feet on the big chair. When the drink spills, he reaches for a napkin and wipes it up.

When it is time to go, Jason lifts him back into the carrier, and he seems happy to get in. We walk some more, heading to the coffee shop where we have been using the Wi-Fi so Jason can upload pictures for our friends and family waiting at home. As soon as we go in, the barista says, "Congratulations!" and smiles at our boy. Jason orders a coffee, and I get my usual smoothie. We get a paper cup and another straw and take Eun-wu

Family Day

out of the carrier again. As soon as he sees the drinks, he climbs onto the booth next to me, stands up and crawls into my lap.

The way to this boy's heart is through his tummy. Amazingly, he is fine the whole time we are at the coffee shop. He pushes the chair around the floor, pleased by the sound it makes on the tiles. When he pushes it back under the table we cheer, "Yay!" and he claps his hands.

We are uneasy about taking him back to the room. We let him push the elevator buttons, and hold the room key. When we go inside, he is like a puppy. Exploring, touching, handling everything. He is so tall we have to move things up where he can't reach them. He is fascinated by the TV.

I try running water into the baby bathtub in the bathroom, but he is not interested. I change his diaper, which he clearly does not like but tolerates with a frown. Jason and I are emotionally and physically exhausted. The prospect of keeping this little one (who is crazy strong!) out of the refrigerator, the TV cords and everything else is daunting. We try saying "no," hesitantly. Wanting to establish boundaries and keep him safe, but not wanting to destroy this fragile trust we have started to build.

The sun is going down. This is the latest Jason and I have stayed up since we've been here. But his normal bedtime is not for two more hours. Lord, give us strength. We lie on the bed and doze in turns while he runs around the room and watches TV. Finally, at 10:00 p.m. almost exactly, he reaches for his bottle, lays himself down on the hard floor and drinks himself to sleep. I scoop him up to put him in the bed with us, but he wakes and pushes away from me. He stands by the bed staring at me, his eyes drooping closed once in a while. He tries pushing me up, and I shake my head "no." Eventually he can't hold his head up anymore, and he stands at the side of the bed with his head down on the mattress. When I try to pull the rest of his body up on the mattress, he scoots away from me and stands by the bed again facing me.

Finally, he puts one foot up on the mattress, his toes pressed against the headboard. Rests his head and torso on the mattress. Then, eventually he puts the other foot up, so that he is lying the wrong way on the bed. I turn off the TV and let him sleep there until I know he is not going to wake up again, and then I sit up, carefully turn him around, and scoot him in between Jason and me under the covers. He has done astoundingly well today. We could never have expected him to do any better than this. I stare at him in the dim light, breathing deeply. This is no baby. I cannot bring myself to even think of him as Hudson. To call him that right now seems unfair. He is Eun-wu still.

GETTING TO KNOW EACH OTHER

September 6: The meeting yesterday was not a wedding day, or hold your newborn baby moment. It was scary, and terribly sad, and confusing. I pray that the Lord will give us strength to make something sweet out of it.

Our boy has slept soundly the entire night. We all did. I am anxious about what today will bring.

He is awake! Sleep lines on his cheeks from the sheets. He's wearing the yellow jammies I picked out for him months ago. I remember holding

them up, trying to picture him in them. So satisfying to actually feel his warm body under that fabric.

He seems confused, but doesn't cry. Sits up on the bed next to Jason looking dazed. I can't imagine what he must be thinking. Did his foster mom tell him about us? How much does he understand? We sent a photo album with all of our pictures in it a few months ago, along with a blue Minky blanket. I'm hoping he has seen our faces before yesterday and understands in some capacity that we are his mom and dad.

His hair is so thin. It lies on his scalp like the bristles of the soft paint brushes I used in kindergarten. He has a pronounced overbite. He sucks in his bottom lip pensively.

I give him a bottle, according to the instructions his foster mom gave us. It is familiar to him. Though he is older than my other children when they transitioned from a bottle to a cup, we want to make as few changes as possible right now.

He carries the bottle around the room chewing on the nipple while he touches and examines everything. When we turn the TV on, he sits on the hard floor, slumped, shoulders rounded, little face turned to meet

the screen squarely, mouth open. I wonder how much of the dialogue he understands.

To prepare for the trip, we practiced a few Korean phrases. We tell him, "gwaenchanh-a," which we were told means "it's okay." I feel clumsy and self-conscious attempting to speak Korean to him.

We continue to say "Oonoo-eh" as DJ You did, guessing that the "eh" at the end must be a diminutive ending, like the "y" in Jonny.

We decide to take him shopping with us since he seems to enjoy riding in the carrier. We feel confident that we know how to navigate the subways now, so we gather his things in a diaper bag, strap him into the carrier and venture out as a family.

I am very aware of people's reactions to us. I watch faces, wondering what they think of these two Americans parading around with a Korean child. I feel like Eun-wu is permitting us to take him with us. Tolerating us. It doesn't feel like taking one of my children on an errand. It feels more like I am escorting a guest around. I want to please him, to convince him that I am worthy to be his mommy.

His face is sober. He is quiet. Bobbing up and down in the carrier. It feels like he is judging it all. It's hard to remember that he is barely a toddler. Just more than a baby. His assessment feels like a collective evaluation, from the entire country of Korea. I want so much to win his approval.

At Namdaemun, we shop the same booths we browsed a few days earlier. Coming back for items we hoped to buy for him. I vacillate between pride that this child (who is obviously different from myself) is mine and a desire to remain inconspicuous. We struggle through the children's clothing store, pointing to him as we ask the vendors if they have his size. No more guessing. He is really here now.

Outside, we see an older woman sitting on a box with crates of edible insects displayed around her. Jason is feeling adventurous, and we approach her. She doesn't appear to notice us even when we are very close. Jason motions toward the displays and asks if he can try one. The woman does not respond at first, and then waves us away, a gesture of dismissal, never even looking at our faces. I try to bite back the embarrassment. Jason shrugs and moves on, unaffected.

We return to the restaurant in the cramped alley and order the same dishes we enjoyed there the first time. As soon as he is relieved of the carrier, Eun-wu crawls confidently into my lap and looks expectantly at the empty table in front of us. I smile. He has claimed me.

He is tall. The top of his head is higher than my chin, so I must peer around him. His body is solid on my lap. He doesn't smell like my baby yet. Funny how important that is to me. I make a note to bathe him tonight so that he will smell familiar to me. Then wonder if that is selfish.

When the food is served, it is a battle to keep his hands out of the dishes. He has obviously never sat in a highchair, or been expected to feed himself his own meal. He digs his chubby fingers into every dish within reach, trying each food happily. Jason is busy pulling the hot soup farther and farther away from him, and I am trying desperately to pinch a few bites with my chopsticks and reach my mouth around this little boy's head.

After more shopping, we buy him bungeoppung, a fish-shaped pancake filled with sweetened red bean paste. He crumbles it in his fists, rolls the pieces between his fingers, sucks on them, picks the pieces

off his tongue, examines them and then starts over. Most of the pastry ends up in my hair and smeared across the carrier, but he is occupied for twenty minutes.

He rarely makes noise. Just watches his environment change, observes us talking to him, buying things, deciphering maps, entering and exiting subways.

At the subway station stairs on the way back to our guest house, a Korean woman walking alone stops us, and with emotion in her voice asks us if we adopted this Korean baby. We answer "yes," guardedly. She tears up and says repeatedly, "Oh, thank you for take care of Korean baby! Thank you!" She strokes Eun-wu's fingers lovingly, nods to us, and smiles joyfully. I am so touched by her approval, but I don't know what to say. She pats his hand

67

with what seems like pride in her people, looking right into his eyes. When we part, I feel warm with gratitude.

Back at our room. More games of predicting what he will try to grab and moving it before he can.

Somehow, he squeezes himself between the headboard and one of the full-length windows. Instinctively, Jason says in a mock surprised voice, "Where did you go?" And begins a game of peek-a-boo. The giggling is such a relief. We did it. We made him laugh. It feels like victory.

His fingers are wrapped around the side of the headboard, and he peeks at us cackling at our gasps of surprise. We continue the game long after we have patience for it. Building a bond with him. His laughter is like our quarry.

Tomorrow is our last day. We leave Seoul at 3:00 p.m. and arrive on the same day at 3:00 p.m. in the United States. Traveling backward through the time zones only adds to the surreal quality of this trip.

SAYING GOODBYE

Today, we take our boy home.

We have packed our things. I am impatient to get home. But nervous to take this little boy on a 14-hour flight. And underneath those emotions is a strange guilt about taking him away from his country. His people. His birth mom. His home.

Is this cruel what we're doing to him? Will he forgive us?

We lay the carrier on the bed, his chubby body on top, and then Jason lifts it onto his back. One last walk before our van comes to take us to the airport. We're going to walk around the neighborhood.

There is a playground with equipment painted green and yellow. It has no fence around it. And there are benches for adults positioned so that they face the play area. Jason lifts Eun-wu out of the carrier and sets him down next to some short metal stairs. He stands with a slumped posture. Somber face. Then suddenly, his expression changes. A group of preschool-age children appears at one end of the playground, and Eun-wu's attention is completely absorbed. With a start, he dodders toward them. His gait is clumsy and awkward. I follow after him with my hands ready to catch him if he stumbles. I am hunched over in an uncomfortable posture. Soon, he is moving quickly after the other children. His face is gleeful! It's as if he's never seen other children before!

He is laughing and chasing after them, choosing any child who passes close to him. The other children pay no attention. They run and play on the equipment, squealing and chattering to each other.

There are teachers or daycare workers supervising the children, and I start to wonder if I should keep Eun-wu away from the class. I lift him and carry him to a display of colorful spinning blocks that are threaded onto a bar. I speak excitedly and try to demonstrate to him how to play with them, but he has no interest at all. He pushes my arms away and clomps toward the other children again laughing with joy. I chase after him tentatively. Look to Jason for guidance, but he shrugs his shoulders.

I am so unsure!

Fifteen minutes later, I feel like I have given him a fair amount of time to play, but I need a break from chasing him. I take his hand and gently lead him back to Jason, expecting a tantrum. To my surprise, he comes calmly, swinging his free arm confidently and panting. This time, once he is strapped into the carrier on my back, instead of leaning away from me, I feel his arms resting on my shoulders, his fingers in my hair. It feels like progress.

In the van, on the way to the airport. There are no seatbelt laws here, and Eun-wu has fallen asleep on Jason's back in the carrier. Jason sits on the

edge of the seat, leaving room for him. His cheek is pressed against Jason's back. His hair is sweaty with sleep.

We are eating at a restaurant in the airport before our flight. We tried taking him out of the carrier when we first arrived, but he refused to hold my hand, and took off in his bumbling stride, stomping in a determined path between strangers. So he is eating bits of our lunch from the safety of the carrier. He seems completely satisfied with this arrangement.

We are waiting at the gate for our flight. We take turns chasing him around. He plops down and removes his shoes anytime we enter a building, so he is tottering around the hall barefoot. We want him to have time to move before we have to be trapped in the airplane for so long.

FLIGHT HOME

Only three and a half hours into our flight. Eun-wu only slept for about an hour. He's been using me as a jungle gym the rest of the time. Climbing on and off my lap, pressing buttons on the remote and calling the flight attendant. Grabbing food out of Jason's dishes. We are finally on our way back to my other babies. I cannot wait to get there.

He is getting tired again. I gave him a tiny piece of Dramamine before we left, and it shouldn't have worn off yet. He is fussing so I take him into the bathroom, change his diaper and put his pajamas on. Then Jason tries to strap him into the carrier but he starts crying. The flight attendant brings him some milk.

We take him out of the carrier but he picks it up and tries to give it to me. He wants me to hold him. He finally falls asleep sitting up on my pillow in my seat. I have to sit forward leaning over my tray table in front of him. When I am sure he is asleep, I move him onto my lap and then try to sleep myself. Doze off and on, with my head cranked over to one side or the other, waking when my neck gets too sore.

He keeps wiggling, sliding down, but he doesn't wake up. There is a man in the next aisle snoring in a concerning way.

I dare not move. I want to stretch this nap out to eat up as much of this flight as possible. It smells like fart in here . . . I wonder if it's Eun-wu's diaper.

The flight attendants come around with snacks. I choose a banana. Nibble on it around his restless head. It is the tiniest banana I've ever eaten. My kids at home would love it.

They are getting up right now. Crawling out of their beds for the last time without us. Grandma and Grandpa probably told them that we are coming home this afternoon. They will get up, get ready, go to Ivan's soccer game, and then head straight up to the Portland airport to meet us.

We are almost to LAX. He has slept almost the entire way on my lap. My body is aching, and I am exhausted. His body slides down gradually, and I have to keep adjusting him so he doesn't fall on the floor. Jason offers to take over, but I am afraid to wake him. So thankful that he is quiet. My tailbone is numb, and my arms tremble with fatigue.

An hour from LAX, I have to go to the bathroom so badly that I am forced to decide what to do with him. I carefully lift him, and try to settle him in Jason's lap, but he wakes up immediately. I sneak off to the bathroom, hoping he will be satisfied with Jason for a few minutes.

Before I leave the bathroom I hear him crying. Embarrassed about the noise, I hurry back to my seat and try to comfort him. I am reluctant to take him back because the freedom to move is such a relief.

The flight attendant hurries over to our seats, leans over and says cheerfully, "Shh shhh shh, baby, it's okay, shh shh." She is obviously troubled by the noise and doesn't want it to bother the other passengers. I start to panic. Lack of sleep and nerves are making my stomach upset. I get right back in line for the bathroom. My time in there is rushed. I return eager to help. Jason is doing his best, but Eun-wu will not be consoled.

The flight attendant leaves and returns with a cup of milk. We pour it into his bottle and he receives it willingly, breathing roughly while he drinks, tears quivering on his cheeks.

Thirty minutes until we land. I am counting them down. He is fully awake now. He has played with every toy, eaten every snack, explored every inch of our seats. I am shivering with anticipation.

At LAX. After standing in line at immigration for so long that we need to repent of our angry attitudes, we have missed our connecting flight. By the time we reach our terminal, the plane is just minutes away from takeoff. We must take another flight that doesn't leave for four hours.

Sweaty and discouraged, we park ourselves in a waiting area with seats that are connected by low tables, and we contact our family and friends

to let them know about the delay. I am frustrated at my lack of patience for chasing Eun-wu around the airport. And I am too tired to carry him anymore.

Sigh. He is asleep again. We spread his blue blanket on the table between our seats and lay him on it. He folds his hands together over his chest as he sleeps. Formally. Like a man pondering.

We are so close to home now. I'm not even nervous about this last flight. Just desperate to get on it.

I yawn and then sigh. And then yawn again.

On our last flight finally. He is wide awake. I fill his bottle and hope it will keep him happy for this short trip. It is evening now. The other passengers are quiet. Some of them are sleeping. We are in the seats closest to the back wall. He sits on Jason's lap popping the lid off of the bottle and then struggling to push it back on. He babbles to me happily. He must think that traveling is his new life.

The closeness of the airplane doesn't seem to bother him at all. He fiddles with my purse strap, chews on the nipple of the bottle. Looks right at us, full eye contact, with an engaged expression. It's new.

We were told that the trauma of the trip home tends to bond the new child with his parents. I think it's true. We've been through a lot already. We are starting to trust each other a little.

We are landing. My heart is full to bursting. I am struggling to keep from crying, but I couldn't say exactly why.

I am going to put this journal away, now.

We made it.

We are home. With Hudson.

And in a matter of minutes, our family will be complete.

At the airport, meeting a new brother and three new sisters.
Hudson was thrilled to see other children.

Meeting Grandpa and Grandma.

Finally home.

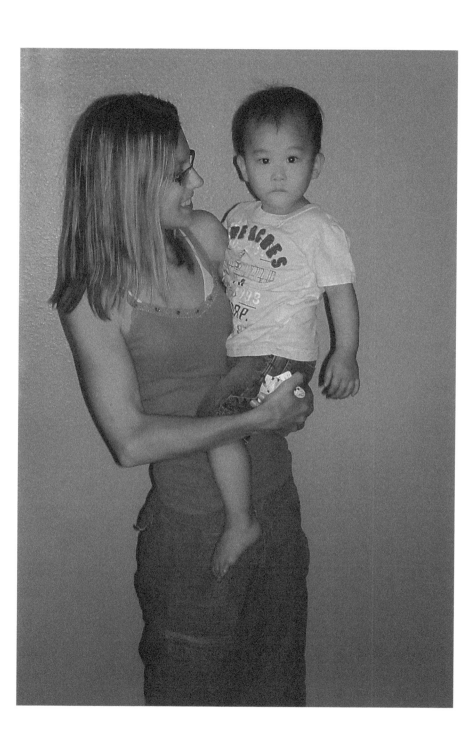

ACKNOWLEDGMENTS

I am incredibly grateful to all of those who encouraged me to write this book, and specifically to those who sacrificed their time puzzling over the details with me: Melanie Jones, Christy Prewette, Heather Timmons, Amy Byler, and Deanna Woodrow. Your gracious help made me believe that anything is possible. Thank you to my parents, Lane and Ruth Clem, for supporting me when I came to you with a crazy idea, and for talking me through the rough spots. Without you, this book would never have been published. Thank you to Holt International for helping us find our son, and to Juhee Park for your infectious enthusiasm and for awakening in us a love for our son's birth country. Thank you to Faith International Adoptions for giving us the opportunity to find number six. And finally, thank you to the women who loved Hudson before I did. I owe you a debt I can never repay.

CPSIA information can be obtained
at www.ICGtesting.com
Printed in the USA
FSHW02n1008040518
47695FS